A DOCUMENTARY HISTORY
OF THE HOLOCAUST™

NAZI CONCENTRATION CAMPS
A POLICY OF GENOCIDE

SUSAN MEYER

ROSEN
PUBLISHING®

New York

Published in 2015 by The Rosen Publishing Group, Inc.
29 East 21st Street, New York, NY 10010

Library of Congress Cataloging-in-Publication Data

Meyer, Susan, author.
Nazi concentration camps: a policy of genocide/Susan Meyer.—First edition.
   p. cm— (A Documentary History of the Holocaust)
Includes bibliographical references and index.
ISBN 978-1-4777-7603-2 (library bound)
1. World War, 1939-1945—Concentration camps—Juvenile literature
2. Holocaust, Jewish (1939-1945)—Juvenile literature. 3. Holocaust, Jewish
(1939-1945)—Influence—Juvenile literature. I. Title.
D805.A2M49 2015
940.53'18—dc23

                                                            2013039223

Manufactured in the United States of America

CONTENTS

INTRODUCTION

A Holocaust survivor speaks at the Auschwitz concentration camp in Poland. His speech was part of the "March of the Living," an annual program that brings thousands of young people to Auschwitz to learn about the Holocaust.

A concentration camp is a place where a large number of people are held as prisoners. Before World War II, the world's only understanding of the term "concentration camp" was as a place where people are held. It might have been a place to hold prisoners of war. Sometimes, refugees from wars or natural disasters were held in camps because they had nowhere else to go. However, today the term "concentration camp" usually refers to the camps that held millions of prisoners in Europe throughout World War II. Unlike those held in a normal jail or prison, people in a concentration camp had not committed a crime and usually had never gone on trial. Instead, the prisoners of these camps were often held because of who they were, not because of what they had done.

Concentration camps were never thought of as a positive place to be. However, in the 1930s and 1940s, as the idea of a concentration camp became more concrete and defined, they were transformed into something even more horrible. When Adolf Hitler and the Nazi Party rose to power in Germany, the Nazis began to systematically round up people they did not want in their country. This included people with different religious beliefs or different politics, or even just people who looked different from them. By far the largest group of people held at concentration camps at this time were Jewish people, mostly from Poland. The camps also held many prisoners of war, Gypsies, homosexuals, Catholic clergy, Polish people, and people with disabilities. These were not just loosely organized prison camps to hold groups of people; this was a large-scale, highly organized system created with the sinister purpose of wiping whole groups of people from the face of the Earth.

The people kept at these camps were treated as less than human. They were transported to the camps in tightly packed cattle cars in the heat of the summer and the cold of the winter. At the camps, they were kept in cramped quarters, without blankets, where disease and pests spread quickly. The food and water they were given often kept them just inches from starvation and dehydration. They were forced to do backbreaking manual labor. Men and women who were too old or too weak to work or children who were too young were murdered en masse. In fact, the Nazis' "Final Solution" was a plan to murder all of the Jews, which involved the creation of a special kind of concentration camp called a death camp. In death camps, people were not kept prisoner; rather, they were murdered, usually in huge gas chambers. The horrors and atrocities seen at these camps were unheard of previously. The Holocaust, as this event in history became known, was an act of genocide—the intentional and organized destruction of an entire group of people—beyond anything the world had seen before. Nearly six million Jewish people were killed during the Holocaust, and an additional five million non-Jewish people were kept as prisoners.

In the course of human history, the events of the Holocaust are relatively recent. Some of the individual men and women who survived life in a concentration camp during the Holocaust are still alive today. However, in another decade or two, we might not have any survivors left to share the tragic, hopeful, and brave stories of triumph from this horrific event. It is therefore crucial that we listen to and record their stories today. There are still acts of genocide seen in places around the world. It is vital that we remember the Holocaust and learn from this tragic period in human history.

CHAPTER 1

WHAT LED TO THE HOLOCAUST?

Looking back today, the atrocities committed during the Holocaust by man against fellow man can be hard to imagine. How did the people of Germany come to allow such things to happen against so many of their neighbors? It is important to understand that these things don't happen overnight. In Germany, the seeds of anti-Semitism were planted long before the 1930s. Anti-Semitism means prejudice or discrimination against Jewish people. As far back as the Middle Ages, Jews were treated differently in Europe. In part because of their differing religious beliefs, they tended to form separate communities in certain cities in Germany. During the First Crusade, around the early 1000s AD, there was a period of persecution of the Jews. Entire communities of people were murdered. Jews were again targeted in the 1300s, when the Black Plague came to Europe. People accused Jews of poisoning the wells and causing the disease. In later centuries, Jewish people were not always allowed equal citizenship across Europe. In some countries, they could only live in Jewish communities. They were also forced to follow certain laws that didn't apply to other people. For example, in the early 1800s, in the city of Frankfurt, Germany, only twelve

This painting by the nineteenth-century French artist Auguste Migette shows the massacre of Jewish people during the First Crusade in the French town of Metz. This massacre occurred in 1096 and was part of a long history of Jewish persecution in Europe.

Jewish couples were allowed to marry every year.

THE WAR TO END ALL WARS

The late nineteenth century brought some new equality for Jewish people living in Germany. However, it was to be short-lived. World War I was fought in Europe between 1914 and 1917. At the time it was called the Great War and the War to End All Wars, but unfortunately all it brought to Europe was death, costly damages, and the seeds of yet another global conflict just two decades later. Many Jewish people fought in the war on both sides. During World War I, twelve thousand German Jews alone were killed fighting for their country.

However, despite these shows of patriotism, many Germans began to accuse the Jews of disloyalty. It was a difficult time for Germany after losing the war, which led to growing tension. In 1916, the German General Staff took a census, or survey, of all Jewish soldiers in the army. The census was publicized widely. It was intended to show that the Jewish soldiers weren't fighting on the front lines as often as other soldiers. The results of the survey showed just the opposite: that the majority of Jewish soldiers were in fact fighting—and dying—on the front lines with everyone else. However, the results of this survey were never published. Instead, the fact that this census was done at all kept the idea that Jews and other Germans were different in people's minds.

The Jews in eastern Europe and Russia who had fought on the other side of World War I didn't fare any better. A quarter of a million of them died fighting for their countries. Over a million more Jewish people became refugees because they were forced from their homes. The czar, or leader of Russia, forced Russian Jews from their homes because he claimed they were helping the Germans. Overall, life for Jewish people all across Europe became much more difficult in the years following World War I.

HITLER'S RISE TO POWER

After World War I, a new political party began to form in Germany. In 1920, its name became the National Socialist German Workers Party, more commonly known as the Nazi Party. The Nazis put out a lot of propaganda to convince citizens that Jews were responsible for Germany's loss in World War I. One of the ideas they spread is that Jews and Marxists (people who follow the communist teachings of Karl Marx) had betrayed the Germans in what became known as the "stab-in-the-back" theory.

Adolf Hitler was a young politician who was a very convincing public speaker. He helped spread the propaganda of

This photo of Adolf Hitler was taken in 1934, shortly after he rose to power and became chancellor of Germany. When Hitler came to power, the swastika, a symbol of the Nazi Party since 1920, became part of the German flag.

the Nazi Party and quickly rose to become the party's leader in 1921. By 1934, Hitler had worked his way past political opposition to become the chancellor of Germany. This gave him total control over Germany and its armed forces. One of his first acts as chancellor was to start a massive increase of the country's army. Hitler also believed in the idea of making the German, or Aryan race, more pure. He made it illegal for non-Jewish and Jewish citizens of Germany to marry each other. He also targeted disabled people and others whom he considered as weakening the Aryan race. As part of eliminating people he didn't want to be part of his country or master race, Hitler and the Nazi Party begun sending people to concentration camps. However, despite the huge death toll that occurred in these camps throughout their history, Hitler is never known to have visited the camps. He also never told people about the killings that went on there.

Under Hitler's government, there was also an increase in anti-Semitism and persecution of Jewish people. Even before they were shipped off to concentration camps, the Nazis created an unpleasant environment for Jews in Europe. In April of 1933, there was an official boycott put in place. People were no longer allowed to shop at Jewish businesses. The reasons given were those spread by Nazi propaganda: that the

Jews had betrayed the Germans during the First World War. On the first day of the boycott, guards stood in front of the doors of Jewish shops or other places of business. They painted the Star of David, an important symbol of Judaism, on Jewish businesses so that German citizens could

In 1933, militiamen in cars bearing the flag of the Nazi Party, like the one seen here, gave speeches in Berlin telling Germans to boycott stores and businesses owned by Jewish people.

recognize them as Jewish and know to take their business elsewhere. This first boycott lasted only one day. However, it

JEWISH GHETTOS

Before Jews were sent to concentration camps, many had seen their rights stripped away while still in their home cities. Many Jewish people in Germany, Hungary, and Poland were required to live in certain parts of cities. They were also required to wear armbands identifying themselves as Jews. The areas where they were rounded up were overcrowded ghettos. The largest of these was the Warsaw ghetto. It was begun in 1940 and kept separate from the rest of the city by a 10-foot (3-meter) wall covered with barbed wire. Nearly four hundred thousand Jewish people lived in the Warsaw ghetto—a space of only 1.3 square

These Jewish children wait in a long line for food at the Warsaw Ghetto in Poland in 1944. Food was scarce in the densely packed ghetto and many went hungry.

miles (3.4 square kilometers). People lived, on average, seven people to a single room.

In a 2003 interview, survivor Lucille Eichengreen describes what life was like in the Polish ghetto in Lodz: "You ate whatever was available, and if you had a friend who would give a bag of potato peels you would wash them at the pump until they were clean, and you would grind them up with a meat grinder. And then you would sort of make a hamburger out of it and you would eat it. Don't ask me what it tastes like. You ate what you had, and if you didn't have anything, you didn't eat. So people died of hunger." Interview courtesy of Telling Their Stories: Oral History Archives Project, the Urban School of San Francisco, www.tellingstories.org.

was a mark of a quickly changing Europe. Soon after, Jews were no longer allowed to hold government jobs, including those of schoolteachers. Then it was not just where they worked, but also where they were allowed to live. Jews were forced to live in overcrowded ghettos that were separated from the rest of the city.

EARLY CONCENTRATION CAMPS

The camp system was set up as a way for the Nazi Party to remove those people they found undesirable from society. In addition to concentration camps where people were held, there were also forced labor camps, death camps, and transit camps, where people were kept when moving to the larger camps. Regardless of type, the living conditions at the camps were always appalling.

The first concentration camps were established in Germany in 1933. One of the earliest camps was called

This photo was taken in 1944 inside prisoner barracks at the Dachau concentration camp. Prisoners were housed in very cramped, poorly ventilated quarters, which led to the spread of disease.

Dachau. Dachau was constructed in an old factory in a small town in southern Germany. It was originally planned as a camp to hold political prisoners. However, the population of the camp would soon grow to include Jews, Gypsies, homosexuals, certain clergymen, and anyone who spoke out against the Nazi Party. After Dachau, camps were constructed as needed and were often temporary structures. More permanent concentration camps were established across Germany, including Oranienburg (near Berlin), Esterwegen (near Hamburg), and Lichtenburg (in Saxony). In Berlin, Germany's capital, prisoners were temporarily held when they were under investigation by the Gestapo. The Gestapo was the secret police employed by the Nazi government, who often decided if people were to be sent off to concentration camps.

In 1934, Hitler directed Heinrich Himmler to create an organized system out of the concentration camps. Himmler was in charge of the Schutzstaffel (German for "protection squad"), or SS guards. The SS was the special guard of the Nazi Party. After 1934, the SS was put in charge of managing all concentration camps. Himmler put another man, Theodor Eicke, in charge of creating a system of management. At the time, Eicke was running Dachau. Eicke created the system that was used for all concentration camps during the Holocaust. This included regulations for how the guards should act and how the prisoners should be treated. Thus the methods used at Dachau became the norm for all concentration camps until they were finally ended in 1945.

EXPANSION OF THE CONCENTRATION CAMP SYSTEM

Between 1938 and 1939, the power of Nazi Germany expanded. Hitler took control of both Austria and

Heinrich Himmler *(right)* is seen here talking to troops in July 1941. Himmler was a right-hand man to Hitler and was instrumental in creating the organized concentration camp system.

Czechoslovakia. In September 1939, he invaded Poland. This led Great Britain and France to both declare war on Germany. Just over twenty years after World War I had ended, World War II had begun.

With the Nazis taking control of other countries in Europe and with the onset of war, the concentration camp system began to expand. There were many new political opponents and others the Nazis hoped to silence by putting them in camps. At the beginning of World War II, there were six concentration camps. Some had been dissolved to make room for larger organizations, and some new camps had been built. The six camps at this time included: Dachau, Sachsenhausen (in Oranienburg, Germany), Buchenwald (near Weimer, Germany), Flossenbürg (in northeastern Bavaria, Germany), Mauthausen (near Linz, Austria), and Ravensbruck (a women's camp near Berlin).

From the early days of the concentration camp system, prisoners were also used for forced labor. With the start of the war and a greater number of prisoners coming into the camps, this became a more organized practice. The original function of concentration camps—to hold political prisoners and other people the Nazis condemned—did not change. However, the SS wanted to expand the use of concentration camps to help with SS construction projects. Location was a critical factor in where the Nazis decided to build new camps after 1937. For example, two concentration camps, Mauthausen and Flossenbürg, were built near large stone quarries. This made it easy to put the prisoners to work mining stone. In some concentration camps, the prisoners themselves built the barracks and buildings that were needed to meet the new wave of prisoners coming in. By 1942, some forced laborers were also helping to make weapons for the German war effort.

Despite the usefulness of concentration camp prisoners as forced labor, Nazis did not value their lives more. They didn't feed the laborers enough for them to survive and often beat

Concentration camps like Mauthausen in Austria were labor camps where prisoners were subjected to inhumane and horrific conditions. The men seen here, photographed after liberation in 1945, were some of the victims of Mauthausen.

or otherwise mistreated them. Many prisoners were worked to death. By the end of the 1930s, concentration camps had transformed. No longer were they just camps where large numbers of prisoners were sent to live. Now they also served as places to hold forced laborers. Some camps also began to appear where prisoners were not meant to be held for long. Called death camps, these camps existed as a place where huge numbers of people were systematically killed.

CHAPTER 2

THE ORGANIZATION OF THE CAMPS

The concentration camp system existed outside of the German state. It was outside of the law. People could be sent to concentration camps as prisoners with a formal charge or without one. There were three different classes of concentration camps. The first, Class I, designated labor camps. Fitter, healthier prisoners were usually sent to these camps. They also held more of the prisoners of war. Class II was similar to Class I except that the treatment was harsher at these camps. The focus was less on the labor the prisoners could produce and more on slowly killing them through mistreatment. Class III comprised the death camps. Prisoners sent to these camps were not to come out alive. The Nazis' ultimate goal was to send all Jews and Gypsies to Class III camps. This was called the Final Solution.

Most camps were built in isolated areas that were close to large cities. This meant that the rest of the world would be less likely to see what was happening in the camps, but that the SS guards could still enjoy big-city comforts. The Nazis built camps away from roads or even access to water. There was plenty of prison labor to build roads and dig wells later. Most sites were made to have enough room for both the SS

The remains of the concentration camp Buchenwald near Weimar, Germany, are seen from above. The grey blocks are actually the former prison barracks where hundreds of thousands of prisoners were kept between 1937 and 1945.

guards and ten thousand to twenty thousand prisoners to stay. The blueprints and maps for many of the camps have been maintained; these primary sources allow people to know more about how the concentration camps were set up and how they changed.

From the maps of Buchenwald, we know the camp had three main areas: the headquarters where operations were run; the SS soldiers' housing; and the compound where the prisoners lived. The barracks for the SS soldiers were built first, and the prisoners would then build their own barracks to stay in. The compound was surrounded by barbed wire to help prevent escape attempts. While images of concentration camps usually show the compound and its simple building structures, the houses that the SS guards lived in were actually very nice. Many had large gardens that were beautifully land-scaped. At Buchenwald, there was even a small zoo for the SS officers where five monkeys and four bears were kept in cages for their amusement. When there were food shortages, the bears were fed from meat rations before the prisoners.

AUSCHWITZ: A MASSIVE ORGANIZATIONAL SYSTEM

In addition to Buchenwald, one of the most well-known con-centration camps is Auschwitz. This camp system was made up of three main camps that used prisoners as forced labor. One of these camps later became Auschwitz II, or Auschwitz-Birkenau, which was an extermination or death camp. The camps were built outside of Krakow in Poland, after it was invaded by the Germans. The first camp, Auschwitz I, was established in May 1940 Auschwitz II was established in the early part of 1942 and Auschwitz III (or Auschwitz-Monowitz) was established later that year.

The control of the Auschwitz camp system demonstrates how carefully the concentration camp system was organized. When Auschwitz I was first built, the SS guards sent prison-ers to clear an area for the camp that was 15.4 square miles (40 sq km). Auschwitz II held the largest total prisoner popu-lation of the three. It contained more than twelve sections of barracks divided from each other by barbed wire. Auschwitz-Birkenau also became a major killing center, as discussed in greater detail in the following section. Auschwitz III, or

This photo shows the heating system between bunk beds in prison barracks at Auschwitz-Birkenau. Part of a network of three camps at Auschwitz, Birkenau was the extermination camp where over one million Jews were killed during the Holocaust.

Auschwitz-Monowitz, was the last established of the three. Its prisoners mostly worked in a nearby rubber plant.

Organizing the management of all three camps was a huge undertaking. Additionally, between 1942 and 1944, there were thirty-nine subcamps created by the SS that were controlled under Auschwitz. Many of these camps were built in the 15.4-square-mile (39.9-square-kilometer) area that had been carved out when Auschwitz I was built. Until 1943, the three concentration camps were controlled as one large complex. The commander of Auschwitz answered to the overall Inspectorate of Concentration Camps, which was an agency of the SS guard main office. In 1943, it was decided that Auschwitz-Birkenau and Auschwitz-Monowitz would become separate, independent concentration camps. Many of the administrative tasks, such as maintaining prisoner records, were still handled in Auschwitz I. A hierarchy of SS guards had to patrol, monitor, maintain records, organize food and water distribution, and maintain labor programs for a population of millions. The concentration camp system was not an accident that slowly evolved. It was a chillingly well-organized and well-staffed machine of destruction.

CONCENTRATION CAMPS TO THE OUTSIDE WORLD

One of the most difficult things to imagine about the concentration camp system is how people could let this happen to their friends and neighbors. Responses to the persecution of Jews ranged from total support of the Nazis to secretly trying to help the Jews, either to escape or to hide. However, the full extent of the concentration camp system and what went on there was kept as tightly hidden as possible by the

"I DON'T LIKE WHAT I SEE"

Gloria Hollander was born in Czechoslovakia in 1930. She was taken from her home, along with her family, when she was only fourteen. She was moved between seven different concentration camps, including Auschwitz, Bergen-Belsen, and Ravensbruck, and she survived all of them. In a 2003 interview, she described what it was like to first arrive in Auschwitz with her father. She described the structure of the camp from the point of view of the prisoners: "It was on a Friday night when we arrived. They kept us locked in all night. The following morning, as daylight broke, Dad looked through the little cracks in the upper right hand corner, there was a little window, but you couldn't see it unless you stood on somebody's back. There was a screen over it. Dad looked through the cracks and that little window, and he was lowered. He said, 'I don't like what I see.' 'There are tall electric wire fences,' Dad said, 'and rows, and rows, and rows, of long barracks.' The name of the place, we later learned, was Auschwitz-Birkenau. This was inside the camp." Interview courtesy of Telling Their Stories: Oral History Archives Project, the Urban School of San Francisco, www.tellingstories.org.

Nazis. Early on, the SS went to great lengths to keep the concentration camp system sounding like a legal system of the state. When a person was taken prisoner, both the prisoner and his or her family were usually told that the imprisonment would be short—just a few months. There were sometimes additional lies that the imprisonment could be shortened by good behavior or that there was a reason for the arrest. Families who made inquiries about a member who had been taken were usually told that he or she was acting up or being rebellious. The Nazis maintained in propaganda that the concentration camps were legitimate

This photo was taken at Theresienstadt, a camp in what is now the Czech Republic that served as a propaganda tool for the Nazis during the war. When the Red Cross sent a group to examine the concentration camp system, Theresienstadt was dressed up to look like a hospitable place.

work camps for political prisoners who were dangerous to the state. They usually convinced (through threats) prisoners to send letters and postcards home talking about how well they were treated.

By the time the Final Solution was underway, the Nazis had to work that much harder to support the fiction that concentration camps were not killing prisoners by the millions. In June of 1944, in an effort to show the world how innocent the camp system was, the Nazis allowed members of the Danish Red Cross, a group devoted to disaster relief, to tour one of their camps. However, the camp the Red Cross toured was not a real concentration camp at all. It was Theresienstadt, a camp in what is now the Czech Republic. The camp was a transit camp. This meant it was usually used as a quick stop on the way to other concentration camps. Before the Red Cross visit, many of the prisoners who had been living temporarily at Theresienstadt were sent to Auschwitz so that it would not look overcrowded. The camp was beautified with new buildings and gardens to make it look like a nicer place to be held prisoner. The Nazis also created a number of cultural activities for the prisoners to take part in to show how well they were treated. So happy were they with the fake camp they had created, that after the Red Cross visit, the Nazis decided to make a propaganda film. The film, called *Theresienstadt*, showed Jewish prisoners looking happy and being well treated by the camp guards. However, the film was just another piece of fiction. Most of the prisoners who appeared in the film were sent off shortly afterward to Auschwitz-Birkenau to be killed.

CHAPTER 3

LIFE AND DEATH IN THE CAMPS

The horrors of life in a concentration camp can be hard to imagine. Starvation, disease, beatings, backbreaking labor, and freezing-cold winters without coats or blankets accounted for the deaths of many prisoners. There was also the day-to-day uncertainty of prisoners never knowing if they would just be rounded up and killed. The harsh conditions of camp life began even before prisoners arrived at camp. Many were prepared for the worst, having heard vague rumors about what went on in concentration camps. Also, most had already suffered mistreatment from the Gestapo and knew whatever lay ahead could not be pleasant.

Most prisoners were arrested in their homes, usually at night. They were then asked questions by the Gestapo. Some prisoners were also beaten or otherwise mistreated as part of the interrogation. Jews especially faced harsh interrogations. Some prisoners were not interrogated at all. Either way the result was almost always the same: prisoners were given red slips by the Gestapo ordering their imprisonment in a concentration camp. After being given a red slip, prisoners might have had to wait a few days or even weeks before they continued their journey to the

This photo, circa 1939, shows the Gestapo arresting a group of Jewish men in a cellar in Poland. It is unknown if the photo represents a genuine arrest or if it was staged as a propaganda tool.

camps. Prisoners were almost always transported in large groups. However, at the rate the Gestapo captured new prisoners, it never took long to form a large group.

The trip to the camps could take many days. Prisoners were crammed as many as 150 people in a single cattle car. Cattle cars are train cars without seats that are really only meant to transport cattle or other nonhuman materials. These cattle cars were usually around 25 feet (7.6 m) by 10 feet (3 m). This means each person had less than 2 square feet (.18 sq m) in which to stand. Due to the overcrowding, hunger and thirst, and lack of sleep, many prisoners died on the journey to the camps. When the doors were opened on the cattle cars, it was not uncommon for several dead bodies to tumble out with the living.

Once prisoners arrived, any personal belongings they had left were taken from them. Family members who had stayed together were often divided. Their hair was cut short, and they were given a uniform to wear. In the Auschwitz concentration camp complex, prisoners were also given a serial number. This number was tattooed on their chest or forearm. Their skin was pierced with a single needle in the

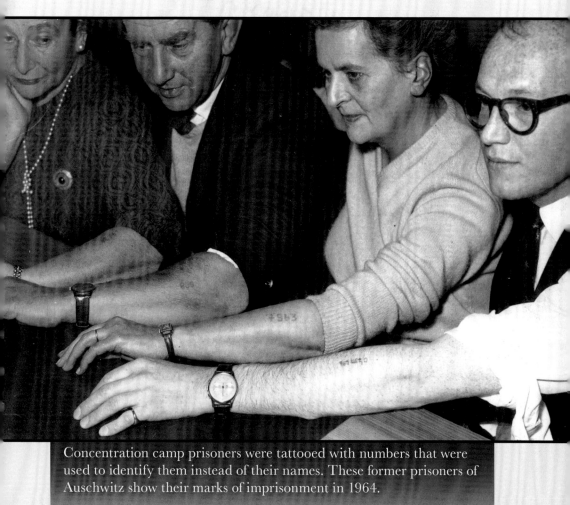

Concentration camp prisoners were tattooed with numbers that were used to identify them instead of their names. These former prisoners of Auschwitz show their marks of imprisonment in 1964.

outline of the numbers, and ink was rubbed into the wound. This was begun in the fall of 1941. Originally, the SS would simply write the prisoner's number on his or her uniform, but so many died and their uniforms were reused, making tattooing the only way to ensure that a prisoner's number died with him or her. More than four hundred thousand serial numbers were assigned at Auschwitz. Only prisoners who were assigned to forced labor ever received serial numbers. Those who were sent to Auschwitz to be killed did not receive numbers or tattoos and were not included in the camp records.

This 1941 photograph shows inmates of the German concentration camp at Sachsenhausen, which held Jewish and political prisoners from 1936 to 1945. The prisoners' thin uniforms were not equipped to handle the harsh winters of northern Germany.

The uniforms of concentration camp prisoners were also marked according to who they were. Beginning in 1938, Jewish prisoners had to wear a yellow star on their uniforms. This was meant to mock the Star of David, an important symbol of the Jewish religion. Jewish prisoners were not the only ones who were identified by their uniforms. Political prisoners were marked with red triangles, Gypsies and those who didn't conform to the Nazi way of thinking wore black or brown triangles, homosexuals wore pink triangles, and Jehovah's Witnesses wore purple triangles. The identifying marks on their uniforms helped the SS guards determine who the people were and why they were imprisoned with just a glance.

DAILY LIFE IN HELL ON EARTH

Life in a concentration camp was very regimented. There was usually a precise schedule maintained. Prisoners would be awakened by whistles early in the morning. They had a half hour to wash, eat, and dress in the black and white striped, ragged uniforms they were given. Breakfast was a piece of stale bread and sometimes a watery coffee. Bread was rationed, and some prisoners got their bread delivered at night instead of the morning. Since they were so hungry, they would eat it immediately, and this meant they received no bread at breakfast time.

In some camps, there was also a half hour of exercise first thing in the morning. This usually consisted of push-ups outside in the snow (in winter) and mud (in summer). Many prisoners caught pneumonia from this type of activity.

Then prisoners were marched in lines to roll call. Roll call could take as long as an hour as every member of every barracks was counted. The morning roll call was done mostly

This February 1941 photograph shows the ritual of roll call at the Sachsenhausen concentration camp in Germany. Prisoners were forced to stand in the snow for hours at a time while their numbers were counted by guards.

as a formality. Few prisoners ever escaped during the night, and all deaths were reported by the prisoner hospital before roll call, so there were seldom any surprises. After roll call, prisoners were commanded to their labor posts. Depending on the camp, work could mean many different things.

In the concentration camps built near quarries, this could mean mining all day for stone. Others contributed to the German war effort by helping to build weapons. Skilled laborers were somewhat more valued. Some prisoners would pretend to be skilled craftsmen because it got them out of more difficult, and often pointless, work. One of the interesting things about the forced labor in the concentration camp system is that despite the availability of this large prison force that was capable of helping the Nazis a great deal, labor was more often used as a punishment than to actually get anything done. Many workers were given frustrating tasks that served no purpose. They would be tasked with constructing a building or a wall without any planning. When the building turned out to be unstable because of this, the next day they would be tasked with taking it down. They were also frequently punished and kept weak by starvation so that any progress they made was very slow.

Prison work continued through the morning and into the afternoon. Prisoners received a half-hour break for lunch. This was their only hot meal of the day. It was usually a thin soup that didn't provide any nutrients. After this lunch, work continued until night.

Then the prisoners were marched back to camp for evening roll call. The evening roll call took longer than the morning one. The prisoners had to stand for hours in the hot sun, during rain or freezing snow, while the SS made sure that no prisoners had escaped during the day. If a single prisoner was missing among thousands, it could lead to even longer delays while the prisoners were all forced to stand at attention. Whenever someone actually managed to escape, the rest of the camp was punished. This punishment was so severe that prisoners discouraged others from escape.

In 1938, two prisoners escaped from Buchenwald in the cold of December. Temperatures were just 5 degrees Fahrenheit (-15 degrees Celsius). The prisoners, all wearing thin uniforms, were forced to stand for roll call all through the night and into the next day—a total of nineteen hours. Over seventy prisoners froze to death. At night, prisoners had only shirts to sleep in, even in the dead of winter, so

A TEENAGER AT AUSCHWITZ

William Lowenberg was born in Germany, and he and his family fled to Holland in the 1930s. William and his family were sent to a concentration camp in Holland called Westerbork. That was the last time William ever saw his family again. At the age of sixteen, he was sent alone to Auschwitz-Birkenau and later to Kaufering in Dachau. In a 2003 interview, William described life at the camp in Kaufering: "You died of starvation, or beatings. Then, of course, the camp had wire around it which was under high voltage all the time and a lot of people went in the wires. In the morning, they had a whole team of lorries they called them, carts, where they picked the bodies and they were burned. The beatings weren't as bad as Auschwitz. They weren't good, the German guards, but we had to work more. There was a purpose of why we worked there, for their war industry. But yes, there were beatings. There certainly was enormous hunger. The hygiene killed a lot of people." Interview courtesy of Telling Their Stories: Oral History Archives Project, the Urban School of San Francisco, www.tellingstories.org.

returning to their bunks after roll call didn't offer much comfort.

SCIENTIFIC EXPERIMENTS

In addition to the regular terrors of daily life at a forced labor camp, some of the largest camps also performed scientific experiments on prisoners. These were carried out in isolated parts of the camps and sometimes in the camp hospitals. These experiments were done by the SS or by scientists who were part of the German air force. Heinrich Himmler was aware of these experiments. Some of them were ordered by

Himmler directly. The worst of these scientific experiments were performed at Dachau, Buchenwald, Auschwitz, Natzweiler (in western France), Ravensbruck, and Sachsenhausen.

The experiments conducted on prisoners fell into three categories. The first included experiments that were intended to help the German war effort. For example, doctors and scientists from the German air force put prisoners in a special chamber that simulated conditions at high altitudes. They wanted to see from what height a person could parachute to safety without being killed by effects from the altitude. The second category of experiments involved trying out new treatments for diseases such as typhus, malaria, tuberculosis, and hepatitis. Prisoners were exposed to the diseases and then tested to see if the medicines worked. Prisoners were also exposed to poisonous gases like mustard gas (a biological weapon used in the war) to test antidotes to it.

The third category of experiments was perhaps the most sinister. These experiments followed the view of the Nazis that the Jews, and others they considered undesirable, were of an inferior race. They did experiments to prove this, including testing to see how different types of people responded to different diseases. Josef Mengele was responsible for many of these experiments at Auschwitz. Mengele's particular interest was in studying twins. He performed abhorrent experiments on Jewish and Gypsy twins, many of them children. Mengele, like many of the so-called "scientists" at the camp, used a staff of trained physicians taken from the prisoner population. These doctors were forced against their will to help in experiments on other prisoners. Much of what we know about Mengele's experiments at Auschwitz comes from one of these prisoner physicians, a man named Dr. Miklos Nyiszli. After the war, he wrote a

Josef Mengele was nicknamed the "Angel of Death" because of the experiments he performed on the prisoners of Auschwitz.

book about his experiences working with Mengele.

THE FINAL SOLUTION

As horrifying as life in the concentration camps could be, one of the worst parts of daily life was that prisoners never knew when it all might end. Death was common in the camps from disease, starvation, and weakening by overwork and harsh temperatures. However, death came even more deliberately starting in 1941. The Germans began to implement what they referred to as the Final Solution. The solution was to the "problem" they saw with Jews existing at all. They wanted to systematically destroy all of the Jewish communities and culture in Europe. They began to do so with extreme efficiency.

In the fall of 1941, Himmler selected an SS general, Odilo Globocnik, to be in charge of putting into place a plan to mass-murder Jews. The plan was referred to with the code name Operation Reinhard. The Nazis began to build killing centers all over Europe, especially in Poland. They created mobile killing stations as well as permanent concentration camps that were really just death camps. Some of these new camps were built exclusively for murder. For example,

Chelmno, Belzec, Sobibor, and Treblinka were camps built in Poland for exactly this purpose. The Nazis also transformed existing concentration camps into killing centers. Majdanek, near Lubin, Poland, became one of these transformed camps. More famously, Auschwitz-Birkenau was reborn as a killing center. More than one million Jews would ultimately be murdered at Auschwitz-Birkenau.

In January of 1942, high-ranking members of the Nazi Party met in Wannsee, a small town outside Berlin. They met to discuss the Final Solution, in what became known as the Wannsee Conference. At the time of this conference, many people already knew about the Final Solution. The purpose of the meeting was not to decide if it should be done, but rather how it should be undertaken. It was a meeting in which men discussed and agreed to the mass murder of Jews not only in areas already under Nazi control, but also of Jews in the United Kingdom and even countries like Switzerland, which had remained neutral during the war. The approximate number of people to be murdered as discussed at the Wannsee Conference numbered eleven million.

The Nazis fine-tuned the easiest and most efficient way to kill large numbers of people. The majority of the prisoners were killed in gas chambers. As prisoners were unloaded from cattle cars, they were told they needed to take showers in order to be disinfected. They were forced into the gas chamber building and the door was locked behind them. They were told to enter the room with their arms up so as many people could fit as possible. The more people in the room, the faster they would suffocate once the room was filled with gas. Once the door was closed, the room was filled with deadly carbon monoxide gas generated from diesel engines. At Auschwitz, the method of gas poisoning was changed due to extensive researching into the most effective way to kill people. At Auschwitz they discovered that Zyklon

Today, the main gas chamber of Auschwitz-Birkenau near Krakow, Poland, contains a memorial to the thousands of men, women, and children whose lives were lost within its walls.

B pellets (previously used in fumigation) created a highly deadly gas when exposed to air. Zyklon gas became the killing method of choice at Auschwitz. Using this method of mass murder, up to six thousand Jews could be killed in a single day.

At these camps, there were usually few barracks or forced labor organizations. Jews were brought not to be imprisoned, but to be killed. There were a few prisoners who were pulled in each new group. These men were required to run the basic operations of these camps. They were required to do tasks like removing bodies from the gas chambers. They also had to bury the dead in mass graves.

LIBERATION

Toward the end of the war, the Allies began to win the battle against the Nazis. As they moved across Europe, the Allies first began to encounter the victims of concentration camps. While there may have been some awareness of what was going on, nothing could prepare these soldiers for what they saw.

The first Allied troops to encounter a concentration camp were from Soviet Russia. Soviet forces reached the concentration camp Majdanek as they marched through Poland in June of 1944. The Germans running Majdanek had not expected the troops so soon. They quickly hurried to destroy evidence of what had gone on in the camp. Majdanek had originally been built as a forced labor camp. However, it was turned into a death camp as part of the Final Solution, and thousands upon thousands of Jews were systematically killed there. As the Soviets approached, the Germans tried to hide this mass murder by destroying the crematorium where the bodies of murdered prisoners had been burned. However, as they rushed to evacuate the camp, they left the gas chambers.

Soviet troops found even more evidence of mass murder when they discovered Auschwitz in January

This photo of the Majdanek extermination camp near Lublin, Poland, shows the road that prisoners took on their final journey to the gas chambers, known as the "Road of Death."

of the following year. Before the arrival of the Soviet soldiers, the Nazis had again tried to remove evidence—in this case, the living prisoners themselves. The majority of the prisoners at Auschwitz had been forced to march west through the cold winter. Most prisoners were weak from hunger, disease, and the conditions of the camp. Many died on these marches, which became yet another tool for mass murder employed by the Nazis. These forced treks became known as death marches. Only a few thousand prisoners remained at the Auschwitz camp complex by

American forces were the first to reach and liberate Dachau. This 1945 photo shows American soldiers stopping some German camp guards.

the time the Soviet soldiers arrived. There still remained much evidence of the over one million people who were killed at Auschwitz. While the Germans had burned many warehouses, the Soviets found some containing prisoners' personal belongings, which suggested the sheer number of prisoners to enter Auschwitz's iron gates. There were also warehouses containing hundreds of suits and dresses as well as hundreds of pounds of human hair. These were all things that had been taken from the prisoners when they arrived at Auschwitz.

THE HORRORS COME TO LIGHT

The testimonies from the liberators of the concentration camps help illustrate just how shocking the discovery of the concentration camps really was. While there were reports of the atrocities that were occurring, they paled in comparison to discovering them in person. Major Cameron Coffman of the 71st Division visited Gunskirchen Lager on the afternoon of May 4, 1945, shortly after it was liberated by American troops. Gunskirchen Lager was a small concentration camp, a subcamp of the larger Mauthausen. Coffman describes the scene that met the American troops: "As we entered the first building the sight that met our startled gaze was enough to bring forth a censorable exclamation from a sergeant who had seen the bloodiest fighting this war has offered. He spat disgustedly on the filthy dirt floor and left the building which was originally built for three hundred but now housed approximately three thousand. Row upon row of living skeletons, jammed so closely together that it was impossible for some to turn over, even if they could have generated enough strength to do so, met our eyes. Those too weak to move defecated where they lay. The place was crawling with lice."

While the Soviet troops were discovering camps in Poland, the American troops were moving across Germany. In April of 1945, American troops found Buchenwald, where more than twenty thousand prisoners, including many children, were being held. American forces went on to liberate prisoners in Dora-Mittelbau, Flossenbürg, Dachau, and Mauthausen.

British forces found and liberated the camps in northern Germany, including the camp Bergen-Belsen, where sixty thousand prisoners were found to be alive. Many of the prisoners were sick with typhus, and one-sixth of them died shortly after liberation.

THE PATH TO RECOVERY

In January of 1945, the SS reported that there were seven hundred thousand prisoners in the concentration camp system. The number of prisoners released during liberation in spring of that year was much smaller. Historians estimate that more than half the concentration camp

This photo shows some of the prisoners, mostly children, of the Dachau concentration camp as the camp was being liberated. Those who were able to stand crowded to the fences to see the soldiers arriving.

deaths during the Holocaust occurred in the last year of World War II.

Liberation was only the first step in a long path to recovery. Many prisoners who were rescued from concentration camps at liberation died shortly after from the results of the experience. The first job of the liberators was to help those who were near starvation or very ill, which amounted to thousands upon thousands of people. As a case in point, of the fifty thousand prisoners released by British troops from the Bergen-Belsen concentration camp in northwestern Germany, twenty thousand were critically ill and thirteen thousand of them died shortly after liberation.

The liberators tried to save as many of the former prisoners as possible. Medical teams were brought in to wash and treat people for parasites and diseases. They treated them with DDT powder, which is a chemical used to kill pests like fleas, lice, and bedbugs. After this, the former prisoners were brought to hospitals that were quickly built in the camps. Doctors made every effort to treat or offer relief for their illnesses—most often pneumonia, dysentery, tuberculosis, and typhus—while also working to readjust their systems to eating food. Many of the prisoners had been starving for so long that their bodies could no longer digest food easily. Doctors had to create special easy-to-digest meals for them as their bodies slowly readjusted to being alive.

CHAPTER 5

A LASTING IMPACT

Although all of the concentration camps in Europe were shut down by the end of May 1945, the impact of the camps was lasting and far-reaching. For the thousands of Jewish and other survivors, coming to terms with life after liberation was difficult. Many of them had to face starting their lives all over again. Some of the survivors were children who had lost their entire families. Others had been separated from their families and sent to different camps. They began the task of searching for loved ones. Their businesses and possessions had all been left behind. They had to figure out a way to start from scratch.

Many survivors, both children and adults, were scared to return to their home countries because of the horrible treatment they had experienced there. Anti-Semitism was also still a problem in Europe—it did not instantly disappear after Germany surrendered. In Poland, there were riots against Jewish people. It was understandable that many survivors were not in a hurry to return to these homes. Unfortunately, that left them with few places to go. Tens of thousands of survivors traveled to parts of western Europe. Here, they were looked after in refugee camps run by British, French, and American troops.

Many countries in Europe closed their borders to Jewish refugees. The United States limited how many Jewish people could emigrate there, as did Britain. Many Jewish people also wanted to emigrate to Palestine, a country in the Middle East that was a site of importance in their religion. In 1948, the State of Israel was officially established in part of Palestine. Jewish refugees quickly began to move to the new country. By 1953, it is estimated that 170,000 Jewish people had moved to Israel. Additionally, in 1947, the United States passed the Displaced Persons Act to allow more refugees to enter the United States. As a result of this act, an estimated

In 1948, when the State of Israel was officially established, thousands of Jewish people, many of them Holocaust survivors, poured into the new country. This circa 1950 photo shows the tents that were set up as temporary housing for the flood of immigrants.

sixty-eight thousand Jews moved to the United States. Many displaced people also moved around the world to other countries, including Australia, Canada, Mexico, New Zealand, and South Africa.

In addition to just finding a place to live safely, survivors had to find a way to deal with the huge emotional losses brought about by the Holocaust. Liberation was a joyful time for many. However, for many it also came too late. By the time the war ended, whole communities had been wiped out. The largest community of Jewish people in Europe had been in Poland. After the war, 90 percent of them had been killed. The Jewish communities in Czechoslovakia and Yugoslavia were also hit with enormous losses. The individual losses on a personal level were even harder to imagine. A survey done by the Organization for Jewish Refugees found that 76 percent of Jewish refugees had lost everyone in their immediate families. Now that they were no longer living just to survive in the camps, these incredible losses became that much harder to deal with. However, slowly but surely, the survivors began picking up the pieces of their former lives. Before the Holocaust in 1933, there were around 9.5 million Jewish people living in Europe. This was 60 percent of the world's total Jewish population at the time. By 1950, the Jewish population of Europe was only 3.5 million people. By this time, only a third of the world's Jewish population lived in Europe, and the majority lived in North and South America. Today, only about 12 percent of Jewish people live in Europe. Instead, the vast majority live in the United States and Israel.

REBUILDING COMMUNITIES

While nowhere near the size of their prewar communities, there are still Jews living in Germany and Poland. Today,

The Treblinka II War Memorial in Poland was completed in 1964. A field of seventeen thousand stones suggests the graves of the nearly one million people killed at the Treblinka II extermination camp. A stone structure in the center is carved with a menorah—a symbol of the Jewish faith—at the top.

there are fewer than five thousand Jews in Poland, living mostly in Warsaw. There are synagogues, places where Jewish people worship, in many cities around the country. Today, Poland seeks to both hold onto the importance of its rich Jewish history and remember how much of that was lost in the horror of the Holocaust. Former death camps Auschwitz-Birkenau, Majdanek, and Treblinka can all be visited as museums and memorials. Additionally, in April of 2013, the Museum of the History of Polish Jewry was opened in Warsaw to help keep this important heritage alive for the people of Poland.

Germany is also home to a Jewish population of about two hundred thousand. In fact, Germany has the ninth-largest Jewish population of any country in the world. Germany has made efforts to increase its Jewish population by making it easier for Jews to immigrate to the country. In 1991, Germany adopted the Contingent Refugee Act. This made it easier for Jews to get German citizenship. While there is no way to change the past, the German government has paid $90 billion to Holocaust survivors since 1952. Germany has also passed laws banning anti-Semitic speech or expression and has made it illegal to deny the existence of the Holocaust. Believe it or not, some people either believe or try to pretend the Holocaust didn't happen. After this law was passed in Germany, it became illegal to spread this idea.

LESSONS OF THE HOLOCAUST

One of the reasons it is important to continue to learn what we can about the Holocaust and the huge and tragic loss of life that occurred is that events of genocide still happen to this day. The Holocaust was something the world had never seen before. The word "genocide" didn't even exist before

ELIE WIESEL: "NEVER FORGET"

Elie Wiesel was fifteen years old when he was sent to Auschwitz with his family. He also spent some time at Buchenwald until the camp was liberated in 1945. He wrote about his experiences

(continued on page 54)

This photo of writer, activist, and professor Elie Wiesel was taken in France in 1989, a few years after he won the Nobel Peace Prize in 1986.

(continued from page 53)

during the Holocaust—including the deaths of all of his family members—in a memoir called *Night*, which was published in 1955. Today, the book has been translated into more than thirty languages. Wiesel has won the Nobel Peace Prize, published more than sixty books, and served as the chairman of the National Holocaust Memorial Council since 1980. He is devoted to making sure that people remember the Holocaust and the millions of victims who were senselessly killed. In addition to this mission, he also works to fight against genocide today. Over the years, Wiesel has supported the causes of groups of persecuted people around the world, including those of the Miskito Indians in Nicaragua, refugees in Cambodia, and victims of genocide in Africa. In a quote that is on permanent display at the U.S. Holocaust Memorial Museum, Elie Wiesel reminds the world of the importance of remembering and of preventing genocide in the future: "Never shall I forget those moments which murdered my God and my soul and turned my dreams to dust. Never shall I forget these things, even if I am condemned to live as long as God Himself. Never."

1944. A Polish Jewish man named Raphael Lempkin created the term to describe the systematic destruction of an entire group of people. The word "genocide" comes from *geno*, which in Greek means "race" or "tribe," and *cide*, meaning "killing." It can be hard to imagine why anyone would ever systematically try to kill off an entire group of people, but the Holocaust is sadly not the most recent occurrence.

In 1990, a war started in Rwanda, a small country in central Africa. The majority of people living in Rwanda were from an ethnic group called the Hutus. In 1994, following the plane crash of the Rwandan president, the Hutus began attacking and killing the minority group, known as the Tutsis. In only one hundred days, somewhere between eight hundred thousand and one million Tutsis were killed. The situation in Rwanda wasn't officially declared to be an act of genocide until after it was over. In 1998, Jean-Paul Akayesu became the first man to be found guilty of genocide. Akayesu was found guilty of crimes against humanity, which he committed while serving as mayor of the Rwandan town of Taba.

A few years later, in 2003, in Sudan, the largest country in Africa, another occurrence of genocide would begin. A western portion of the country, an area called Darfur, contained six million people from a number of different ethnic, racial, and religious backgrounds. In this ongoing crisis, many local people were killed and even more were displaced by a militia group called the Jangaweed. In 2004, the U.S. government declared the situation in Darfur to be genocide. This was the first time the word had been applied to a situation as it was happening.

Sadly, genocide is not a problem that was left behind when the concentration camps were liberated in Europe. However, there is hope to be found as more people learn about these situations and as governments start taking action sooner.

LEARNING ABOUT THE HOLOCAUST WHERE YOU LIVE

Many of the former concentration camps that were not destroyed were made into museums for people to visit. These include Auschwitz, Dachau, and Buchenwald. These museums and others around Europe are an important reminder of

Donald A. McCarthy, a veteran of World War II, tours the U.S. Holocaust Memorial Museum in Washington, D.C. Holocaust museums and memorials have been created around the world and are an incredibly important part of making sure people remember and learn about this dark time in our human history.

the tragedies that occurred there. However, not all Holocaust museums are abroad. There are more than forty institutions and memorials in the U.S. and Canada for people to learn about these events. One of the largest is the U.S. Holocaust Memorial Museum in Washington, D.C.

In addition to museums, organizations called Shoah Foundations are dedicated to helping people remember and honor the Holocaust. *Shoah* is the Hebrew word used to describe the Holocaust. There are currently two Shoah foundations active around the world. One is the Survivors of the Shoah Visual History Foundation established in 1994. This nonprofit has interviewed and recorded hundreds of survivors of the Holocaust about their experiences. Taping and cataloguing these stories and experiences is incredibly important, especially as more time elapses between the Holocaust and the present. In the next two decades, there will likely not be any survivors of the Holocaust left to tell their stories. Having them forever alive in these recordings will ensure that people in the future never forget. The second Shoah Foundation was founded in 2000 in France. It is called the Foundation pour le Memoire de la Shoah, which means "the Foundation for Remembering the Shoah." It is equally dedicated to projects furthering the research, history, and education of the Holocaust for future generations.

In 1951, Israel created a holiday called Yom Hashoah to commemorate the Holocaust. The date chosen for this holiday is a date that comes from the Hebrew calendar, and it usually falls in April or May. This date marks the anniversary of the uprising at the Warsaw ghetto. In 1980, the U.S. Congress declared that a Day of Remembrance for the Holocaust should be observed in the United States as well. The U.S. Day of Remembrance is observed on the same day as Yom Hashoah each year. In 2005, the United Nations also established a date to remember the Holocaust, which is known as International Holocaust Remembrance Day. Unlike Yom Hashoah and the United States's Day of Remembrance, this is a fixed day falling on January 27 each year. January 27, 1945, was the day that troops liberated the concentration camp Auschwitz-Birkenau.

In the United States, the Day of Remembrance was created to commemorate the millions of lives lost during the Holocaust due to the systematic destruction and persecution of Jews and others by the Nazis. Every year for the week around the Day of Remembrance, the U.S. Holocaust Memorial Museum has a reading of the names of many of the victims of the Holocaust as a way to show respect to the victims and survivors. This can be attended by anyone at the museum and is broadcast on the museum's Web site.

For those who don't have a Holocaust memorial or museum nearby, there are many ways to honor and commemorate the Day of Remembrance. Schools and libraries can create displays recognizing the true scope and mass scale of the Holocaust or invite a Holocaust survivor to speak about his or her experiences. Book clubs and film viewings on the subject of the Holocaust are also good ways to learn about and discuss this tragic time. Some suggestions for books to read and discuss are *Number the Stars* by Lois Lowry, *The Boy in the Striped Pajamas* by John Boyne, and *The Devil's Arithmetic* by Jane Yolen.

However one chooses to honor those who were senselessly murdered during the Holocaust, the important thing is to simply remember them. Passing on the facts and personal histories of the Holocaust and its survivors will help people to never forget this tragic period of human history.

Timeline

January 30, 1933 Adolf Hitler becomes the official chancellor of Germany.

March 20, 1933 The first concentration camp, Dachau, is opened.

April 1, 1933 Germany declares a legal boycott on all Jewish shops and businesses.

July 12, 1936 Sachsenhausen concentration camp is opened in Oranienburg, Germany.

July 15, 1937 Buchenwald concentration camp is opened outside of Weimar, Germany.

March 5, 1939 German troops invade Czechoslovakia.

September 1, 1939 World War II officially begins in Europe when Germany invades Poland.

April 27, 1940 Heinrich Himmler orders construction to begin on the Auschwitz camp.

November 24, 1941 The Theresienstadt camp is opened. It will later be used as a propaganda piece by the Nazis when it is visited by the Red Cross.

December 8, 1941 The first killing operations begin at Chelmno in Poland, as part of the Final Solution.

December 11, 1941 Nazi Germany declares war on the United States.

January 20, 1942 Germans at the Wannsee Conference discuss implementation of the Final Solution.

March 17, 1942 Murder of Jews begins in Belzec extermination camp.

April 19, 1943 A major uprising begins in the Warsaw ghetto in Poland.

January 17, 1945 Prisoners are forced to evacuate Auschwitz in the beginning of a death march.

January 27, 1945 Soviet troops liberate the prisoners of Auschwitz.

April 11, 1945 Prisoners at Buchenwald stage an uprising. They are liberated by American troops later that day.

April 29, 1945 American troops liberate the prisoners of Dachau concentration camp.

May 7, 1945 Germany surrenders to the Allies, with the exception of the Soviet Union.

May 9, 1945 Germany surrenders to the Soviet Union.

Glossary

ANTI-SEMITISM Prejudice or discrimination against Jewish people.

ARYAN The term the Nazi Germans used to describe non-Jewish individuals of Nordic and Germanic descent.

ATROCITY An extremely cruel act.

CENSUS A survey of a population.

CHANCELLOR The highest leader in Germany.

CONCENTRATION CAMP A place where a large number of prisoners are held, especially referring to camps during World War II where millions of people, mostly Jewish, were mistreated and killed.

DYSENTERY A disease that affects the intestines and can be fatal if untreated.

EXTERMINATION CAMP A Nazi-run camp where prisoners were sent to be killed; sometimes called a death camp.

FINAL SOLUTION An organized plan by Nazi Germany to systematically murder all of the Jews in Europe.

GENOCIDE The systematic murder of an entire group of people.

GESTAPO The secret police in Nazi Germany.

GHETTO A part of a city away from the rest of the population where Jews were forced to live in the 1930s and 1940s; ghettos were usually very overcrowded.

LIBERATION The act of setting free from imprisonment.

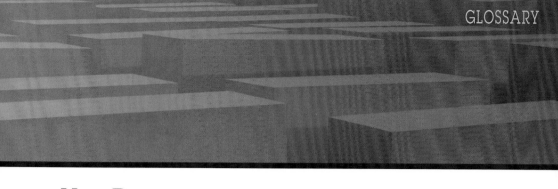

NAZI PARTY The National Socialist German Workers Party; the political party run by Hitler.

POLITICAL PRISONER A person who is imprisoned for his or her political beliefs or actions.

PROPAGANDA Information that is intentionally biased and misleading.

REFUGEE A person who is forced to leave his or her home country; a displaced person.

SHOAH The Yiddish word for the Holocaust; also the name of a foundation helping to honor and remember it.

SS GUARD Standing for Schutzstaffel, this was the protective army of the Nazi Party. It also ran the concentration camps.

SYNAGOGUE A place where Jewish people go to worship.

TYPHUS A deadly disease spread by lice, ticks, fleas, and other pests.

For More Information

Auschwitz-Birkenau Memorial and Museum
Więźniów Oświęcimia 20
32-603 Oswiecim
Poland
Web site: http://www.auschwitz.org.pl
This museum and memorial contains the former concen-
tration camp Auschwitz I as well as the death camp
Auschwitz-Birkenau. Visitors can take a guided tour
of the original grounds where millions of Jews were
both imprisoned and killed.

Buchenwald and Mittelbau-Dora Memorials Foundation
99427 Weimar
Germany
+49 (0) 3643-430-0
Web site: http://www.buchenwald.de/en
The mission of this foundation is to preserve the memorial sites at the Buchenwald concentration camp and
that of its sub-camp, Mittelbau-Dora. The foundation
organizes a number of educational exhibitions on the
history of the camp as well as cultural events on the
national and international levels.

Dachau Concentration Camp Memorial
Pater-Roth-Str. 2a
D - 85221 Dachau
Germany

+49-8131-66-99-70
Web site: http://www.kz-gedenkstaette-dachau.de
On the site of the former Dachau concentration camp
    now sits a memorial that visitors can tour to learn
    about the history of Dachau. A former camp mainte-
    nance building now houses a museum that focuses on
    the stories of individual prisoners.

Elie Wiesel Foundation for Humanity
555 Madison Avenue
New York, NY 10022
(212) 490-7788
Web site: http://www.eliewieselfoundation.org
Founded by Elie Wiesel and his wife, Marion, soon after
    he won the Nobel Peace Prize in 1986, this founda-
    tion fights injustice and intolerance by facilitating
    dialogue. It centers on youth programs, including an
    annual essay contest open to college students.

Europen Shoah Legacy Institute
Rytirska 31
110 00 Praha 1
Czech Republic
+420 224 186 242
Web site: http://www.shoahlegacy.org
This public benefit institution was founded to seek resti-
    tution for the cultural property stolen from Jewish

people by the Nazis during World War II, provide
social welfare to Holocaust survivors, and promote
Holocaust education, research, and remembrance.

Montreal Holocaust Memorial Centre
5151, Chemin de la Côte-Sainte-Catherine
Montréal, QC H3W 1M6
Canada
(514) 345-2605
Web site: http://www.mhmc.ca/en
Through its permanent collection of videos, testimonies,
artifacts, and information about the Holocaust, this
museum and memorial seeks to guide people of all
ages in learning about difficult subjects, including
anti-Semitism, genocide, and the Holocaust.

USC Shoah Foundation
650 West 35th Street, Suite 114
Los Angeles, CA 90089-2571
(213) 740-6001
Web site: http://sfi.usc.edu
This organization focuses on teaching about the
Holocaust and other incidents of genocide by record-
ing interviews with survivors and witnesses. Since
1994, the foundation has gathered 51,696 audio-
visual testimonies in 32 different languages, all of
which are available through its online archives.

U.S. Holocaust Memorial Museum
100 Raoul Wallenberg Place SW
Washington, DC 20024-2126
(202) 488-0400
Web site: http://www.ushmm.org
This museum stands as a source of information about
the events of the Holocaust as well as a memorial to
those who lost their lives during the tragic event. In
addition to its permanent and temporary exhibits, the
museum also maintains an archive of video, interviews, and timelines from the period.

Vancouver Holocaust Education Centre
950 41 Ave W
Vancouver, BC V5Z 2N7
Canada
(604) 264-0499
Web site: http://www.vhec.org
Founded in 1983 by Holocaust survivors, this Canadian
teaching museum and leader in Holocaust education
helps more than fifteen thousand students each year.
In addition to exhibits, the museum also runs school
programs and maintains an archive of information
about the Holocaust on its Web site.

Wiener Library for the Study of the Holocaust and Genocide
29 Russell Square

London WC1B 5DP
UK
+44 (0)20 7636 7247
Web site: http://www.wienerlibrary.co.uk
Formed in 1933, the Weiner Library has one of the most
    extensive collections of books and artifacts on the
    Holocaust and Nazism. The library's collection
    includes published and unpublished works, press
    cuttings, photographs, and personal testimonies.

WEB SITES

Due to the changing nature of Internet links, Rosen
Publishing has developed an online list of Web sites related
to the subject of this book. This site is updated regularly.
Please use this link to access the list:

http://www.rosenlinks.com/DHH/Camps

For Further Reading

Bannister, Nonna, and Carolyn Tomlin. *The Secret Holocaust Diaries: The Untold Story of Nonna Bannister.* Highland Ranch, CO: Tyndale House Publishers, 2009.

Baxter, Ian. *Himmler's Nazi Concentration Camp Guards.* South Yorkshire, England: Pen and Sword Books, 2013.

Bergen, Doris L. *War and Genocide: A Concise History of the Holocaust.* Plymouth, England: Rowman and Littlefield Publishers, 2009.

Boyne, John. *The Boy in the Striped Pajamas.* New York, NY: Random House, 2006.

Browning, Christopher R. *Remembering Survival: Inside a Nazi Slave Labor Camp.* New York, NY: W. W. Norton, 2010.

Darring, Gerald. *Jewish Experience of the Holocaust: In Their Own Words.* Mobile, AL: Wilhelm Publishing House, 2013.

Engelking, Barbara, and Jacek Leociak. *The Warsaw Ghetto: A Guide to the Perished City.* Ridgewood, NJ: Sheriden Books, 2009.

Fulbrook, Mary. *A Small Town Near Auschwitz: Ordinary Nazis and the Holocaust.* Oxford, England: Oxford University Press, 2012.

Kenez, Peter. *The Coming of the Holocaust: From Anti-Semitism to Genocide.* Cambridge, England: Cambridge University Press, 2013.

Kiernan, Ben. *Blood and Soil: A World History of Genocide and Extermination from Sparta to Darfur.* New Haven, CT: Yale University Press, 2009.

Langbein, Hermann. *Against All Hope: Resistance in the Nazi Concentration Camps.* St. Paul, MN: Paragon House, 2009.

Lipiner, Lucy. *Long Journey Home: A Young Girl's Memory of Surviving the Holocaust.* Bloomington, IN: iUniverse, 2013.

Lower, Wendy. *Hitler's Furies: German Women in the Nazi Killing Fields.* New York, NY: Houghton Mifflin Harcourt, 2013.

Lowry, Lois. *Number the Stars.* New York, NY: Houghton Mifflin, 1989.

Michalczyk, John J. *Filming the End of the Holocaust.* London, England: Bloomsbury Academic, 2014.

Montague, Patrick. *Chelmno and the Holocaust: The History of Hitler's First Death Camps.* Chapel Hill, NC: The University of North Carolina Press, 2012.

Radio, Lucyna B. *Between Two Evils: The World War II Memoir of a Girl in Occupied Warsaw and a Nazi Labor Camp.* Jefferson, NC: McFarland & Company, 2008.

Selg, Peter. *From Gurs to Auschwitz: The Inner Journey of Maria Krehbiel-Darmstädter.* London, England: Rudolf Steiner Press, 2013.

Shaw, Martin. *Genocide and International Relations: Changing Patterns in the Transitions of the Late Modern World.* Cambridge, England: Cambridge University Press, 2013.

Shephard, Ben. *After Daybreak: The Liberation of Bergen-Belsen, 1945.* New York, NY: Random House, 2005.

Suderland, Maja. *Inside Concentration Camps: Social Life at Extremes.* Cambridge, England: Polity Press, 2013.

Venezia, Shlomo. *Inside the Gas Chambers: Eight Months in the Sonderkommando of Auschwitz.* Malden, MA: Polity Press, 2011.

Wachsmann, Nikolaus, and Jane Caplan. *Concentration Camps in Nazi Germany.* Oxford, England: Routledge, 2010.

Waller, James E. *Becoming Evil: How Ordinary People Commit Genocide and Mass Killing.* New York, NY: Oxford University Press, 2007.

Weiss-Wendt, Anton. *Racial Science in Hitler's New Europe (1938-1945).* Lincoln, Nebraska: University of Nebraska Press, 2013.

Whitlock, Flint. *Buchenwald: Hell on a Hilltop.* Brule, WI: Cable Publishing, 2013.

Wiesel, Elie. *Night.* New York, NY: Hill and Wang, 1972.

Yolen, Jane. *The Devil's Arithmetic.* New York, NY: Penguin, 1990.

Zullo, Allan. *Escape: Children of the Holocaust.* New York, NY: Scholastic, 2009.

Bibliography

Baxter, Ian. *Himmler's Nazi Concentration Camp Guards (Images of War)*. South Yorkshire, England: Pen & Sword Books, 2013.

Baxter, Ian. *The SS of Treblinka*. London, England: The History Press, 2010.

Beorn, Waitman Wade. *Marching into Darkness: The Wehrmacht and the Holocaust in Belarus*. Cambridge, MA: Harvard University Press, 2013.

Bergen, Doris L. *War and Genocide: A Concise History of the Holocaust*. Plymouth, England: Rowman and Littlefield Publishers, 2009.

Bernard, Jean. *Priestblock 25487: A Memoir of Dachau*. Bethesda, MD: Zaccheus Press, 2010.

Deem, James M. *Auschwitz: Voices from the Death Camp*. Berkeley Heights, NJ: Enslow Publishers, 2011.

Eichengreen, Lucille. Interview with Julianne, Leah, Matthew, and Howard Levin. Telling Their Stories Project, May 30, 2002. Retrieved July 1, 2013 (http://tellingstories.org/holocaust/leichengreen/index.html).

Engelking, Barbara, and Jacek Leociak. *The Warsaw Ghetto: A Guide to the Perished City*. Ridgewood, NJ: Sheriden Books, 2009.

Fleming, Michael. *Auschwitz, the Allies and the Censorship of the Holocaust*. Cambridge, England: Cambridge University Press, 2014.

Goldhagen, Daniel Jonah. *Hitler's Willing Executioners: Ordinary Germans and the Holocaust*. New York, NY: Vintage Books, 1996.

Gutman, Yisrael, and Michael Berenbaum. *Anatomy of the Auschwitz Death Camp*. Bloomington, IN: Indiana University Press, 1994.

Hett, Benjamin Carter. *Burning the Reichstag: An Investigation into the Third Reich's Enduring Mystery*. New York, NY: Oxford University Press, 2013.

Kiernan, Ben. *Blood and Soil: A World History of Genocide and Extermination from Sparta to Darfur*. New Haven, CT: Yale University Press, 2009.

Kinderblock 66: Return to Buchenwald. Directed by Rob Cohen. Interviews with Naftali-Duro Furst, Pavel Kohn, Israel-Laszlo Lazar, and Alex Moskovic. 2012. Film.

Klee, Ernst. *"The Good Old Days": The Holocaust as Seen by Its Perpetrators and Bystanders*. New York, NY: Simon and Schuster, 1991.

Kogen, Eugene. *The Theory and Practice of Hell*. New York, NY: Farrar, Straus, and Giroux, 2006.

Lifton, Robert Jay. *The Nazi Doctors: Medical Killing and the Psychology of Genocide*. New York, NY: Basic Books, 1988.

Lowenberg, William. Interview with Oral History Class, Howard Levin, and Deborah Dent Samake. Telling Their Stories Project, April 3, 2003. Retrieved July 1, 2013 (http://tellingstories.org/holocaust/wlowenberg/index.html).

Lower, Wendy. *Hitler's Furies: German Women in the Nazi Killing Fields*. New York, NY: Houghton Mifflin Harcourt, 2013.

Lyon, Gloria Hollander. Interview with Katie Rose B., Whitney L., Jonny M., and Howard Levin. Telling Their Stories Project, May 16 and 31, 2002.

Retrieved July 1, 2013 (http://tellingstories.org/
holocaust/glyon/index.html).

MacLean, French L. *The Camp Men: The SS Officers Who
Ran the Nazi Concentration Camp System.* Atglen, PA:
Schiffer Publishing, 1998.

Marcuse, Harold. *Legacies of Dachau: The Uses and Abuses
of a Concentration Camp.* Cambridge, England:
Cambridge University Press, 2001.

Montague, Patrick. *Chelmo and the Holocaust: The History of
Hitler's First Death Camps.* Chapel Hill, NC: The
University of North Carolina Press, 2012.

Nyiszli, Miklos, and Tibere Kremer. *Auschwitz: A Doctor's
Eyewitness Account.* New York, NY: Arcade Publishing, 1960.

Radio, Lucyna B. *Between Two Evils: The World War II
Memoir of a Girl in Occupied Warsaw and a Nazi Labor
Camp.* Jefferson, NC: McFarland & Company, 2008.

Ranz, John. *Inhumanity: Death March to Buchenwald.*
Bloomington, IN: AuthorHouse, 2007.

Shephard, Ben. *After Daybreak: The Liberation of Bergen-Belsen,
1945.* New York, NY: Random House, 2005.

U.S. Army. *Dachau: 1945 Army Reports from the Nazi
Concentration Camp.* Athens, GA: Red and Black
Publishers, 2009.

U.S. Holocaust Memorial Museum. "Concentration
Camp System: In Depth." *Holocaust Encyclopedia.*
Retrieved July 24, 2013 (http://www
.ushmm.org/wlc/en/article.php?ModuleId
=10007387).

Venezia, Shlomo. *Inside the Gas Chambers: Eight Months in the Sonderkommando of Auschwitz.* Malden, MA: Polity Press, 2011.

Waller, James E. *Becoming Evil: How Ordinary People Commit Genocide and Mass Killing.* New York, NY: Oxford University Press, 2007.

Weiss-Wendt, Anton. *Racial Science in Hitler's New Europe (1938–1945).* Lincoln, NE: University of Nebraska Press, 2013.

Index

R

Ravensbruck, 19, 26, 37
Red Cross, 28
refugee camps, 48
refugees, 10, 49–50
religion, 5
Russia, 10, 42
Rwanda, 54–55

S

Sachsenhausen, 19, 37
Schutzstaffel (SS), 17, 19, 21–23,
    25, 26, 32, 33, 35, 36, 38, 46
scientific experiments, 36–38
Shoah Foundations, 57–58
Sobibor, 39
South Africa, 50
Star of David, 12, 33
starvation, 29, 35, 36, 38, 47
Sudan, 55
survivors, 6, 15, 26, 48, 50, 52,
    57–58, 59
Switzerland, 39

T

Theresienstadt, 28
transit camps, 15, 28
Treblinka, 39, 52

U

United Kingdom, 39
United Nations, 58
United States, 49–50, 54, 55,
    57, 58
    Day of Remembrance, 58–59
    Displaced Persons Act, 49–50
U.S. Holocaust Memorial
    Museum, 54, 57, 58

W

Wannsee Conference, 39
weather, 29, 35, 38, 43
Westerbork, 36
Wiesel, Elie, 53–54
women's camp, 19
World War I, 9–10, 18

Y

Yom Hashoah, 58
Yugoslavia, 50

Z

Zyklon B, 39–41

ABOUT THE AUTHOR

Susan Meyer is the author of a number of young adult non-fiction books. She is a firm believer that remembering even the most troubled parts of human history is a way to help us better inform our future. Meyer currently lives in Queens, New York, with her husband, Sam, and her cat, Dinah.

PHOTO CREDITS